AN IMAGINATION LIBRARY SERIES

WORLD'S LARGEST

SNAKES

Anacondas

by Valerie J. Weber

Gareth Stevens Publishing

A WORLD ALMANAC EDUCATION GROUP COMPANY

Please visit our web site at: www.garethstevens.com
For a free color catalog describing Gareth Stevens Publishing's
list of high-quality books and multimedia programs,
call 1-800-542-2595 (USA) or 1-800-387-3178 (Canada).
Gareth Stevens Publishing's fax: (414) 332-3567.

Library of Congress Cataloging-in-Publication Data available upon request
from publisher. Fax (414) 336-0157 for the attention of the Publishing
Records Department.

ISBN 0-8368-3653-7

First published in 2003 by
Gareth Stevens Publishing
A World Almanac Education Group Company
330 West Olive Street, Suite 100
Milwaukee, WI 53212 USA

Text: Valerie J. Weber
Cover design and page layout: Scott M. Krall
Series editor: Jim Mezzanotte
Picture Researcher: Diane Laska-Swanke

Photo credits: Cover © Brian Kenney; p. 5 © Joe McDonald/Visuals Unlimited;
p. 7 © James P. Rowan; pp. 9, 21 © François Gohier/Ardea London Ltd.; p. 11
© Keith & Liz Laidler/Ardea London Ltd.; p. 13 © M. Watson/Ardea London Ltd.;
p. 15 © Jim Clare/naturepl.com; p. 17 © Francois Savigny/naturepl.com; p. 19
© C. P. George/Visuals Unlimited

Printed in the United States of America

1 2 3 4 5 6 7 8 9 07 06 05 04 03

Front cover: **As a green anaconda climbs down this tree on the Amazon River, it pushes its belly into the smooth trunk to get a firm grip.**

TABLE OF CONTENTS

Words that appear in the glossary are printed in **boldface** type the first time they occur in the text.

The Winner by Weight

In the contest for the largest snake in the world, the green anaconda wins. This anaconda can grow to be over 30 feet (9 meters) long — as long as a school bus! Another kind of snake, the reticulated python, can grow to be longer, but the green anaconda is heavier and wider and can be up to 3 feet (1 m) around its middle. So scientists usually declare the green anaconda to be the largest snake in the world.

The green anaconda and its smaller cousin, the yellow anaconda, live in **tropical** South America. Green anacondas also live on Trinidad, an island located off the coast of Venezuela in South America.

This anaconda is keeping its body warm by lying in the sunshine. Giant snakes such as anacondas all live in tropical areas.

How Large Can an Anaconda Grow?

No one knows for sure how large anacondas can grow, because, unlike you, snakes never stop growing. The largest anaconda ever seen may have measured nearly 62 feet (19 m) long. Scientists argue over whether an anaconda could really have been this long. Some scientists think a snake that large would have difficulty supporting its own weight.

Gigantic snakes are often very old. We do not know how long anacondas can live in their natural **habitats**. In the zoo, they can survive for twenty years or more. But you do not see many anacondas in zoos. They are hard to care for because they are bad tempered and do not feed well.

The giant anaconda is sometimes called the green anaconda so people do not confuse it with its smaller cousin, the yellow anaconda.

Colored for Camouflage

Most anacondas, especially the big ones, must lie waiting for their **prey** to go past them. The snakes are just too big to move fast! An anaconda has skin that matches its surroundings. This **camouflage** helps it to remain hidden from its prey.

The giant anaconda is green with black splotches. These spots get lighter on its belly, which is yellow green. Its **scales** are glossy and smooth.

An anaconda's nostrils and eyes are higher on its head than on most snakes. With its nostrils and eyes up high, an anaconda can wait in the water, unseen by passing animals.

This anaconda is hiding in tree roots to survive the dry season. An anaconda can go a long time without eating.

Waiting in the Water

Anacondas usually stay in swamps, slow-moving rivers and streams, or near the shallow banks of lakes. The water helps support their giant bodies and keeps them hidden from their prey, who come to the edge of the water to drink.

No one knows for sure how long anacondas can stay underwater — they may be able to stay under the water anywhere from five to thirty minutes. Unlike many snakes, anacondas have room in their thick bodies for two lungs, allowing them to take big breaths and hold them.

Anyone for a swim! Like many snakes, anacondas swim by using an "S"-shaped motion. Notice the curves in this anaconda's body.

Patience Pays Off

An anaconda waits hours or even days for its prey. It grabs its prey and wraps the animal in its strong **coils**. Then, it drags the animal into the water. Anacondas eat many kinds of animals, including capybaras (large **rodents**) and **reptiles** such as the caiman (a kind of small alligator).

Some people tell stories about anacondas eating very large animals, such as cattle! These stories are a little true and a little false. An anaconda has jaws that stretch open very wide and a body that can expand, so it can eat prey that is much larger than its own width. The cattle these giant snakes eat, however, are usually young and small.

Anacondas have been known to feed on large animals, such as wild pigs and deer. This anaconda is about to eat an iguana, a much smaller prey.

A Mouth Like a Rubber Band

The jaws of an anaconda are joined at the back by a strong **tendon** that stretches. The tendon lets the anaconda open its mouth so wide that the opening is larger than its head.

An anaconda's jaws have four different parts that move separately from each other, helping the snake "walk" its mouth over its prey. The anaconda has about a hundred teeth, but it does not chew its food. Instead, the anaconda uses its teeth to move its meal down its **flexible** throat. It also uses a lot of spit to make swallowing easier.

A snake can stick its tongue through a notch in its upper jaw. Using this notch, a snake can stick out its tongue without opening its mouth!

Are These Stories True?

For many years, people have told tales of monster anacondas **lurking** in swamps. In 1944, workers exploring for oil in Colombia, South America, shot an anaconda. After dragging it to dry land, they measured it and found it to be 37.5 feet (11.4 m) long. They later discovered the snake had recovered enough to swim or crawl away!

In 1910, someone claimed to have shot a 54-foot (16-m) giant snake along the Jivari River in Peru, South America. Scientists have reported seeing anacondas 30 to 35 feet (9 to 11 m) long.

This team of scientists carries a 16-foot (4.9-m) female anaconda. The man at the front grasps the snake tightly behind the head to keep it from biting him.

No Family Life

In their natural habitats, male and female anacondas **mate** in the spring and then never see each other again. Female anacondas are pregnant for six to seven months. During this time, they do not eat at all! One possible reason the female anacondas do not eat is to make sure they do not get hurt from hunting prey.

A large female anaconda gives birth to about seventy baby snakes. These youngsters weigh from 8 to 9.5 ounces (227 to 269 grams). When they are born, they slip away from their mother. They are ready to hunt and eat on their own, without any help from their parents.

These four-week-old baby anacondas are twisted together in a big heap. See how many heads you can find!

Giants in Danger

Even though anacondas can eat people, they usually do not. Instead, they swim away at the first sign of danger. Anacondas that are in **captivity** are usually the ones that injure or kill people. With its inward-curving teeth, the anaconda can deliver a sharp and nasty bite!

People do kill anacondas, often because they are afraid of the snakes. As people build farms and homes close to jungle rivers and swamps, they destroy the habitats of anacondas. Like all the giant snakes, anacondas are a **threatened species**. Fortunately, people are now working to save the places where anacondas live.

This young anaconda wraps itself around a man's hand. Anacondas are protected in zoos, but their rain forest habitats are being destroyed.

MORE TO READ AND VIEW

Books (Nonfiction)   *Anacondas. Animals of the Rain Forest* (series). Christy Steele
                        (Raintree/Steck-Vaughn)
                        Anacondas. Naturebooks Reptiles and Amphibians (series).
                        Mary Ann McDonald (Child's World)
                        Anacondas. Predators in the Wild (series). Anne Welsbacher
                        (Capstone Press)
                        Anacondas. Snakes (series). James E. Gerholdt (Checkerboard Library)
                        Anacondas. Snakes (series). Linda George (Capstone Press)
                        Fangs! (series). Eric Ethan (Gareth Stevens)

Books (Fiction)   *Dance Y'All.* Bettye Stroude (Marshall Cavendish Corp.)
                        I Need a Snake. Lynne Jonell (Putnam Publishing Group)
                        Snake Camp. George Edward Stanley (Golden Books)

Videos (Nonfiction)   *Amazing Animals Video: Scary Animals.* (Doris Kindersley)
                        Henry's Amazing Animals: Rainforest Animals. (Doris Kindersley)
                        Land of the Anaconda. (National Geographic)
                        Predators of the Wild: Snakes. (Warner Studios)
                        Spiders and Snakes. (Simitar Video)

PLACES TO WRITE AND VISIT

Here are three places to contact for more information:

Black Hills Reptile Gardens
P.O. Box 620
Rapid City, SD 57709
USA
1-800-355-0275
www.reptile-gardens.com

Indianapolis Zoo
1200 W. Washington St.
Indianapolis, IN 46222
USA
1-317-360-2001
www.indyzoo.com

**Rainforest Reptile
Refuge Society**
1395 176th St.
Surrey, British Columbia
Canada V3S 9S7
1-604-538-1711
www.rainforestsearch.com/rrrs

WEB SITES

Web sites change frequently, but we believe the following web sites are going to last. You can also use good search engines, such as **Yahooligans!** [www.yahooligans.com] or **Google** [www.google.com], to find more information about anacondas. Here are some keywords to help you: *anacondas, rain forest snakes, reptiles,* and *South American snakes.*

www.bio.davidson.edu/Biology/herpcons/ Myths/Modern_Myths.html
Do snakes hypnotize their victims? Do they travel in pairs? At this site, you will learn what is fact and what is fiction!

www.enchantedlearning.com/subjects/ reptiles/snakes/Anacondacoloring.shtm/
The drawing of an anaconda at this web site needs your artistic touch. Print it out and put your crayons to work.

www.extremescience.com/ BiggestSnake.htm
Visit *Biggest Snake* to see a great photograph of an anaconda.

www.nashvillezoo.org/anaconda.htm
Anaconda, from the Nashville Zoo's web site, has a neat photograph of an anaconda. It also tells you how this giant snake got its name.

www.rainforestsearch.com/rrrs/ snk_ya.htm
The Rainforest Reptile Refuge Society takes care of unwanted pets, including anacondas. Visit this page from the society's web site to see great photographs of a yellow anaconda. It was donated to the society when it was a baby, because its owner did not know how to care for it.

GLOSSARY

You can find these words on the pages listed. Reading a word in a sentence helps you understand it even better.

camouflage (CAM-uh-flahj) — patterns and colors that make something look like part of its surroundings, so it is hard to see 8

captivity (kap-TIH-vuh-tee) — kept in a closed space, either as a pet or in a zoo 20

coils (KOYLZ) — the circles a snake can form with its body 12

flexible (FLEK-suh-buhl) — able to bend easily without breaking 14

habitats (HAB-uh-tatz) — places where an animal or plant lives 6, 18, 20

lurking (LERK-eeng) — waiting in a place, hidden from view 16

mate (MAYT) — come together to make some babies 18

prey (PRAY) — animals that are hunted by other animals for food 8, 10, 12, 14, 18

reptiles (REP-TYLEZ) — animals such as lizards and snakes that usually have scaly skin and either short legs or no legs 12

rodents (RO-dentz) — small furry animals, such as mice, with large front teeth 12

scales (SKAYLZ) — small, stiff plates, made mostly of the same material as human hair and nails, that cover a snake's skin 8

tendon (TEN-duhn) — a strong, flexible band of tissue that attaches a muscle to a bone 14

threatened species (THRET-end SPEESH-eez) — plants or animals of a certain kind that are in danger of dying out 20

tropical (TROP-ih-cull) — being in a part of the world where the temperature is always warm and plants usually grow year-round 4

INDEX